AF265162

ABSTRACT

The propagation of plane waves in a stratified ionosphere is considered. It is shown that the construction of 'true' characteristic waves depends upon the diagonalization of a matrix by a Loewy transformation. For a homogeneous ionosphere this construction can always be carried out explicitly. For the general case we obtain the wave solution in terms of characteristic waves which have the properties usually attributed to characteristic waves in magneto-ionic theory. In addition, the interaction between these waves is made clear by the introduction of continuous reflection and transition coefficients. Ordinary and extraordinary wave-reflection levels are shown to be points at which the elementary divisors of a certain matrix become non-simple. Complicated expressions are obtained from which ionospheric reflection and transmission coefficients may be obtained explicitly.

Explicit solutions are obtained for normally incident waves with an oblique earth's magnetic field and for oblique incident waves with a vertical earth's magnetic field.

<u>ERRATA</u>

<u>page</u>	<u>line</u>	<u>Change</u>		
Table of Contents	Section IV-A	Equation	to read	Solution
6	2 below Eq.(3.6)	where	"	we have used the notation
	3 below Eq.(3.7)	$\exp(i\frac{\omega}{c}\lambda + z)$	"	$\exp(i\frac{\omega}{c}\lambda_+ z)$
8	Eq.(4.3)	$W(z) = \Omega \ldots$	"	$W(z) = \underset{\xi}{\overset{z}{\Omega}}$
9	Eq.(4.6)	$U(z) = \Omega \ldots$	"	$U(z) = \underset{\xi}{\overset{z}{\Omega}} \ldots$
	10 and 9 from bottom	...carried out for various ionospheric configuration.	"	...carried out explici for various ionospheric configurations.
	8 from bottom	Omit 'may'		
	7 and 6 from bottom	existence	"	construction
13	Eq.(4.17)	$\exp\int_{z_o}^{x}[(r_{ij} \ldots$	"	$\exp\int_{z_o}^{x}[(r_{ii} \ldots$
16	2 from bottom	$z' \leq z \leq$"	"	$z' \leq z \leq z$"
40	right side of Eq.(I.4)	$\underset{z_o}{\overset{z_o}{\Omega}}$	"	$\underset{z}{\overset{z_o}{\Omega}}$

TABLE OF CONTENTS

Page

- 1 -

1. Introduction

The linearized theory of ionospheric propagation may be separated into
three parts: determination of the electron and ion distributions, derivation
of the electromagnetic properties of the ionosphere, and solution of the re-
sulting Maxwell's equations. While all of these problems have received con-
siderable attention, the last one has not been advanced to a point comparable
to that of tne first two. That is, the Maxwell's equations which contain the
most accurately determined tensor properties of the ionosphere have not been
fully examined.

Approximate solutions of Maxwell's equations can be obtained by the methods
of geometrical optics, or, when separation of variables is applicable, the so-
called " wave" solutions may be determined. Some of the experimental ob-
servations are not adequately accounted for by the geometrical optics solutions. Therefore we must either correct the geometrical optics solutions
by including higher-order terms in the asymptotic expansion, or seek accurate
wave solutions. The latter alternative shall be considered in Part I of the
present paper. The problem of finding these wave solutions would entail first
an investigation of the separation of Maxwell's equations with tensors ε, μ
and σ appropriate for the ionosphere. However, we will consider a horizontally stratified medium and seek "plane wave" solutions; for this case the
problem can immediately be reduced to finding the solution of a system of
ordinary differential equations. These separated equations can then be solved
by the extended Peano-Baker method described in a companion report [2].

The form of the solution for an arbitrary inhomogeneous anisotropic
medium is seen to justify the form of solution which is assumed by some
authors at the start of their investigations. In the neighborhood of a
turning point, the solution indicates the extent to which the four "characteristic"
waves are coupled. From the general formulation of the problem it is easy to

determine sufficient conditions for the complete uncoupling of the 'ordinary' and 'extraordinary' waves.

More specific formulations for various combinations of the earth's magnetic field and incident wave directions are considered in Part II. Two of these cases, (1) normal incidence with an oblique magnetic field, and (2) oblique incidence with a vertical magnetic field, are then solved by the method of analysis given in Part I.

PART I. GENERAL IONOSPHERIC THEORY

2. Formulation

We consider a plane ionosphere with horizontally stratified properties in the layer $z_0 \leq z \leq z_1$. The exterior of this region is assumed to be free space extending to infinity in both directions. If we suppress the time factor $e^{-i\omega t}$, Maxwell's equations for this composite medium become

$$\nabla \times \vec{E}(x,y,z) = i \frac{\omega}{c} \vec{H}(x,y,z)$$

(2.1)

$$\nabla \times \vec{H}(x,y,z) = -i \frac{\omega}{c} \vec{K}(z) \, \vec{E}(x,y,z).$$

Here the magnetic permeability has been taken as unity throughout. The space and the tensor dielectric properties, $\vec{K}(z)$, are as follows.

For the ionosphere $(z_0 \leq z \leq z_1)$:

$$(2.2) \quad \vec{K}(z) \equiv \left(k_{ij}(z) \right) \equiv \begin{pmatrix} 1 - A(\delta^2 - y_1^2) & A(y_1 y_2 + i\delta y_3) & A(y_1 y_3 - i\delta y_2) \\ A(y_1 y_2 - i\delta y_3) & 1 - A(\delta^2 - y_2^2) & A(y_2 y_3 + i\delta y_1) \\ A(y_1 y_3 + i\delta y_2) & A(y_2 y_3 - i\delta y_1) & 1 - A(\delta^2 - y_3^2) \end{pmatrix}.$$

For free space $(z \leq z_0 \text{ and } z \geq z_1)$

$$(2.3) \quad \vec{K}(z) \equiv I, \text{ the unit matrix.}$$

The derivation of the above dielectric tensor (2.2) is well known and has been carried out in a rigorous form by van der Wyck [3]. The ionospheric model assumed is that of free space containing a distribution, $N(z)$, of free electrons with charge ε and mass m. These electrons collide with heavier particles with average collisional frequency $\nu(z)$ and are in the presence of an external static magnetic field $\vec{H}_E(z)$ due to the earth. The notation used in equation (2.2) is related as follows to the above quantities and to the usual notation: we have defined

$$\delta(z) \equiv 1 - i\,\frac{\nu(z)}{\omega} \equiv 1 - i\,Z(z)$$

(2.4)
$$(y_1, y_2, y_3) \equiv \frac{\varepsilon}{m\omega c}\,\vec{H}_E(z) \equiv \vec{Y}(z)$$

$$A(z) \equiv \frac{4\pi\varepsilon^2 N(z)}{m\,\omega^2}\;\frac{1}{\delta(\delta^2 - Y^2)} \equiv X(z)\,\frac{1}{(1-iZ)\left[(1-iZ)^2 - Y^2\right]}\;.$$

The major problem is to find the solution of Maxwell's equations (2.1) which has a specified behavior at infinity namely, in general, that it be an outgoing wave, as is insured by the Sommerfeld radiation condition. This field arises from a given source or distribution of sources (usually a dipole specified by a condition analogous to Sommerfeld's). The discontinuity conditions for electromagnetic fields must be satisfied at the planes $z = z_0$ and $z = z_1$. Such a solution may be constructed by first obtaining plane wave solutions of equation (2.1) which have the required continuity and outgoing properties, and the integrating over all possible orientations to produce the required source. In the present paper our main problem will be that of obtaining such plane wave solutions.

If cylindrical coordinates are used in the previous formulation, equations (2.1) and (2.3) remain unchanged but the matrix $(k_{ij}(z))$ of equation (2.5) is altered (see [3], Chap. V). In this case cylindrical wave solutions would be sought and they could be superposed to construct the field due to an arbitrary source. A cursory examination of this problem has shown that only in the case of vertical earth's magnetic field may cylindrical wave solutions be obtained by separation of variables.

3. Generalized Transmission Line Equations

The electromagnetic field components which satisfy equations (2.1) are divided into longitudinal and transverse fields by calling the direction of increasing z the "transmission" direction. Thus $E_3(x,y,z)$ and $H_3(x,y,z)$, the z-components of the electromagnetic field, comprise the longitudinal field and the remaining components are the transverse field. From Maxwell's equations (2.1), the longitudinal field may be obtained algebraically in terms of the transverse field and some transverse derivatives. This yields

$$E_3 = \frac{-ic}{\omega k_{33}}\left[\frac{\partial H_2}{\partial x} - \frac{\partial H_1}{\partial y}\right] - \frac{k_{31}}{k_{33}}E_1 - \frac{k_{32}}{k_{33}}E_2$$

(3.1)

$$H_3 = \frac{ic}{\omega}\left[\frac{\partial E_2}{\partial x} - \frac{\partial E_1}{\partial y}\right].$$

In the remaining Maxwell equations the longitudinal field may be eliminated by using the above expressions; thus,

$$\frac{\partial E_1}{\partial z} = \frac{-i\omega}{c}H_2 - \frac{ic}{\omega k_{33}}\left[\frac{\partial^2 H_2}{\partial x^2} - \frac{\partial^2 H_1}{\partial y \partial x}\right] - \frac{k_{31}}{k_{33}}\left[\frac{\partial E_1}{\partial x}\right] - \frac{k_{32}}{k_{33}}\left[\frac{\partial E_2}{\partial x}\right]$$

$$\frac{\partial H_2}{\partial z} = \frac{-i\omega}{c}\left(k_{11} - \frac{k_{31}k_{13}}{k_{33}}\right)E_1 - \frac{i\omega}{c}\left(k_{12} - \frac{k_{32}k_{13}}{k_{33}}\right)E_2 - \frac{ic}{\omega}\left[\frac{\partial^2 E_2}{\partial y^2} - \frac{\partial^2 E_2}{\partial y \partial x}\right]$$

(3.2)

$$- \frac{k_{13}}{k_{33}}\left[\frac{\partial H_2}{\partial x} - \frac{\partial H_1}{\partial y}\right]$$

$$\frac{\partial H_1}{\partial z} = \frac{i\omega}{c}\left(k_{21} - \frac{k_{31}k_{23}}{k_{33}}\right)E_1 - \frac{i\omega}{c}\left(k_{22} - \frac{k_{32}k_{23}}{k_{33}}\right)E_2 - \frac{ic}{\omega}\left[\frac{\partial^2 E_1}{\partial y \partial x} - \frac{\partial^2 E_2}{\partial x^2}\right]$$

$$+ \frac{k_{23}}{k_{33}}\left[\frac{\partial H_2}{\partial x} - \frac{\partial H_1}{\partial y}\right]$$

$$\frac{\partial E_2}{\partial z} = \frac{i\omega}{c} H_1 - \frac{ic}{\omega k_{33}} \left[\frac{\partial^2 H_2}{\partial y \partial x} - \frac{\partial^2 H_1}{\partial y^2} \right] - \frac{k_{31}}{k_{33}} \left[\frac{\partial E_1}{\partial y} \right] - \frac{k_{32}}{k_{33}} \left[\frac{\partial E_2}{\partial x} \right] \quad .$$

This linear second-order system of partial differential equations involves only the transverse field, and from their solution the longitudinal field can be computed using equations (3.1). Applying the method of separation of variables to the system (3.2) it is found that there exist solutions of the form

$$\vec{E}(x,y,z) = \vec{V}(z)\, e^{\,i\,\frac{\omega}{c}(px+qy)}$$

(3.3)

$$\vec{H}(x,y,z) = \vec{I}(z)\, e^{\,i\,\frac{\omega}{c}(px+qy)} \quad .$$

These solutions may be interpreted as plane waves whose orientation is determined by the arbitrary parameters p and q. Alternatively, by a slight extension of ordinary terminology, we may say that a particular choice of p and q determines a particular "mode" . Of course in the present case there is a continuum of modes, rather than a discrete set, as occur in some electromagnetic problems.

The equations for the determination of $V(z)$ and $I(z)$ are obtained by substituting equations (3.3) in equations (3.1) and (3.2):

$$V_3(z) = \frac{-1}{k_{33}(z)} \left[pI_z(z) - qI_1(z) + k_{31}(z)V_1(z) + k_{32}(z)V_2(z) \right]$$

(3.4)

$$I_3(z) = \left[p\, V_2(z) - qV_1(z) \right]$$

and

$$\frac{ic}{\omega}\frac{dV_1}{dz} = \left[p\,\frac{k_{31}}{k_{33}} \right]V_1 - \left[1 - \frac{p^2}{k_{33}} \right]I_2 - \left[\frac{pq}{k_{33}} \right]I_1 + \left[p\,\frac{k_{32}}{k_{33}} \right]V_2$$

(3.5)

$$\frac{ic}{\omega}\frac{dI_2}{dz} = \left[q^2 - k_{11} + \frac{k_{31}k_{13}}{k_{33}} \right]V_1 + \left[p\,\frac{k_{13}}{k_{33}} \right]I_2 - \left[q\,\frac{k_{13}}{k_{33}} \right]I_1 - \left[pq + k_{12} - \frac{k_{32}k_{13}}{k_{33}} \right]V_2$$

$$\frac{ic}{\omega}\frac{dI_1}{dz} = \left[pq + k_{21} - \frac{k_{31}k_{23}}{k_{33}} \right]V_1 - \left[p\,\frac{k_{23}}{k_{33}} \right]I_2 + \left[q\,\frac{k_{23}}{k_{33}} \right]I_1 - \left[p^2 - k_{22} + \frac{k_{32}k_{23}}{k_{33}} \right]V_2$$

$$\frac{ic}{\omega}\frac{dV_2}{dz} = \left[q\frac{k_{31}}{k_{33}}\right]V_1 + \left[\frac{pq}{k_{33}}\right]I_2 + \left[1 - \frac{q^2}{k_{33}}\right]I_1 + \left[q\frac{k_{32}}{k_{33}}\right]V_2.$$

These equations may be considered generalized transmission line equations (see the treatment of Maxwell's equation in isotropic media [4]). As such, they represent a three-wire non-uniform transmission line whose distributed parameters depend upon the frequency of the impressed voltage.

The problem formulated in Section 2 has now been reduced to that of solving the transmission line equations (3.5) with the appropriate $k_{ij}(z)$ (given by equations (2.2) and (2.3)) in each region. The discontinuity conditions associated with Maxwell's equations are satisfied in the present case if the transverse field components are continuous, i.e., if

$$(3.6) \qquad \left[V_1(z),V_2(z),I_1(z),I_2(z)\right]_{z=a-o}^{z=a+o} = 0.$$

Here $z = a$ is any level at which there is a discontinuity of the medium and where

$$\left[f(x)\right]_{x=a_-}^{x=a_+} \equiv f(a_+) - f(a_-).$$

The Sommerfeld radiation condition which is to apply in the free space above the ionosphere, $z \geq z_1$, becomes

$$(3.7) \qquad \begin{aligned} &\lim_{z\to\infty} \left| \frac{\partial V_j(z)}{\partial z} - i\frac{\omega}{c}\lambda_+ V_j(z)\right| = 0 \\[2mm] &\lim_{z\to\infty} \left| \frac{\partial I_j(z)}{\partial z} - i\frac{\omega}{c}\lambda_+ I_j(z)\right| = 0 \end{aligned} \qquad , \quad j = 1,2.$$

Here λ_+ is the as yet unspecified propagation constant. This condition ensures that at infinity the field components behave like

$$\exp\left(i\frac{\omega}{c}\lambda_+ z\right)$$

and thus represent upgoing waves.

Below the ionosphere, $z \leq z_0$, we shall not impose a radiation condition but, rather, specify the incident electric or magnetic field amplitudes at some level, say $z = 0$. Thus for $j = 1$ and 2 we require either

$$(3.8a) \qquad \left[\frac{\partial V_j(z)}{\partial z} + i \frac{\omega}{c} \lambda_- V_j(z) \right]_{z=0} = 2i \frac{\omega}{c} \lambda_- A_j \, ,$$

or

$$(3.8b) \qquad \left[\frac{\partial I_j(z)}{\partial z} + i \frac{\omega}{c} \lambda_- I_j(z) \right]_{z=0} = 2i \frac{\omega}{c} \lambda_- B_j \, .$$

Here λ_- is again the propagation constant and the A_j and B_j are the amplitudes of the transverse waves incident upon the ionosphere. The conditions (3.7) and (3.8a) or (3.8b) together with the continuity requirement are sufficient to ensure uniqueness of the solution. The mode synthesis could proceed only after the problem formulated above has been solved.

4. Solution of Transmission Line Equations

The analysis is simplified by introducing the column and square matrices $W(z)$ and $A(z)$ respectively, defined by

$$(4.1a) \qquad W(z) = \begin{pmatrix} w_1(z) \\ w_2(z) \\ w_3(z) \\ w_4(z) \end{pmatrix} = \begin{pmatrix} V_1(z) \\ I_2(z) \\ I_1(z) \\ V_2(z) \end{pmatrix} \, ,$$

and

$$(4.1b) \qquad A(z) = \begin{pmatrix} \left[-p \frac{k_{31}}{k_{33}}\right] & \left[1 - \frac{p^2}{k_{33}}\right] & \left[\frac{pq}{k_{33}}\right] & \left[-p \frac{k_{32}}{k_{33}}\right] \\[2mm] \left[-q^2 + k_{11} - \frac{k_{31}k_{13}}{k_{33}}\right] & \left[-p \frac{k_{13}}{k_{33}}\right] & \left[q \frac{k_{13}}{k_{33}}\right] & \left[pq + k_{12} - \frac{k_{32}k_{13}}{k_{33}}\right] \\[2mm] \left[-pq - k_{21} + \frac{k_{31}k_{23}}{k_{33}}\right] & \left[p \frac{k_{23}}{k_{33}}\right] & \left[-q \frac{k_{23}}{k_{33}}\right] & \left[p^2 - k_{22} + \frac{k_{32}k_{23}}{k_{33}}\right] \\[2mm] \left[-q \frac{k_{31}}{k_{33}}\right] & \left[-\frac{pq}{k_{33}}\right] & \left[-1 + \frac{q^2}{k_{33}}\right] & \left[-q \frac{k_{32}}{k_{33}}\right] \end{pmatrix} \, .$$

The generalized transmission line equations (3.5) can now be written in matrix form as

$$(4.2) \qquad \frac{d}{dz} W(z) = i \frac{\omega}{c} A(z)W(z).$$

This system is solved by the extended Peano-Baker method described in a previous report [2]. A summary of the definitions and identities necessary are included for convenience in Appendix I of the present report. The solution of the system (4.2) is

$$(4.3) \qquad W(z) = \Omega \left\{ A(x) \right\} W_o$$

in any of the regions described by equations (2.2) and (2.3). Here ξ and z must lie in the same region and W_o is the value of $W(\xi)$. In the present section we shall confine our attention to the ionosphere, taking $\xi = z_o$ and $W_o = W(z_o)$. The solutions for other regions are considered in Section 6.

The wave behavior and other expected features of the solution are not contained in the present form (4.3). To remedy this situation we introduce, four new dependent variables $u_i(z)$, defined as

$$(4.4) \qquad \begin{pmatrix} u_1(z) \\ u_2(z) \\ u_3(z) \\ u_4(z) \end{pmatrix} \equiv U(z) = P^{-1}(z)W(z), \quad \text{or}$$

$$W(z) = P(z)U(z).$$

Here $P(z)$ is an arbitrary non-singular 4x4 square matrix with inverse $P^{-1}(z)$ and elements $p_{ij}(z)$; $i,j = 1,2,3,4$. Thus the $u_i(z)$ are linear combinations, with non-constant coefficients, of the $w_j(z)$, and vice versa. From equations (4.3) and (4.4) the equation satisfied by $U(z)$ is derived:

$$(4.5) \qquad \frac{dU}{dz} = \left[i \frac{\omega}{c} P^{-1}(z)A(z)P(z) - P^{-1}(z) \frac{dP}{dz} \right] U(z).$$

- 9 -

$$(4.6) \qquad U(z) = \Omega \left\{ i \frac{\omega}{c} P^{-1}AP - P^{-1}\dot{P} \right\} U_o,$$

where

$$\dot{P}(z) \equiv \frac{dP}{dz} \quad \text{and} \quad U_o = P^{-1}(z_o)W_o.$$

However, since $P(z)$ is arbitrary we may attempt to choose it such that the
solution (4.6) has some of the desired features.

If two square matrices $L(z)$ and $M(z)$ are related such that for some
non-singular matrix $P(z)$,

$$P^{-1}(z)L(z)P(z) - P^{-1}(z)\dot{P}(z) = M(z),$$

then they are said to be equivalent in the sense of Loewy [6]. Thus if $i \frac{\omega}{c} A(z)$
is equivalent in the sense of Loewy to a diagonal matrix $\Lambda(z)$ then from (4.6)
and (I.2) (see Appendix I) we see that each $u_i(z)$ would be the exponential
integral of the i-th diagonal element of $\Lambda(z)$. Such a solution represents
'true' characteristic waves whose existence has been considered by Booker [5]
and others. If the medium were homogeneous, A and P would be constant and
hence $\dot{P}$ would equal 0; thus the Loewy transformation would reduce to the
ordinary similarity transformation $P^{-1}AP$. In this case the conditions for
diagonalization are well known [7] and indeed diagonalization may be carried
out for various ionospheric configuration. This is in conformity with the
accepted theory that 'true' characteristic waves may exist in a homogeneous
ionosphere. However, in the general ionospheric case the existence of the
diagonalizing Loewy transformation and hence the existence of 'true' characteristic waves remain open questions.

Perhaps the next best simplifying choice of $P(z)$, as suggested above
for the homogeneous case, is that in which

$$(4.7) \qquad P^{-1}(z)A(z)P(z) = \Lambda(z) \equiv \left(\lambda_i(z)\delta_{ij} \right),$$

which is a diagonal matrix. Such a $P(z)$ always exists and can be easily obtained if the eigenvalues, $\lambda_i(z)$, of $A(z)$ are distinct, i.e., if there are no repeated roots of the characteristic equation

$$(4.8) \qquad |\lambda I - A(z)| = 0.$$

This algebraic equation will be shown to be the well-known fourth-degree equation of magneto-ionic theory. The inequality of the roots of this equation is a sufficient but not necessary condition for (4.7) to hold. The more general requirement is that the matrix $(\lambda I - A(z))$ have simple elementary divisors [7]. This distinction will be recalled in Section 6 where it is of importance; but for the present we assume the eigenvalues to be distinct. The solutions $u_i(z)$ given by (4.6) and corresponding to $P(z)$ taken to satisfy (4.7), where the eigenvalues are distinct, are called characteristic waves.

To examine the form of these characteristic waves we introduce the notation

$$(4.9) \qquad \left(r_{ij}(z)\right) \equiv - P^{-1}(z)\,\dot{P}(z).$$

Next, the coefficient matrix of the system (4.5) is split into a diagonal matrix and a zero-diagonal matrix as follows:

$$(4.10) \qquad D(z)+N(z) \equiv \left[i\,\frac{\omega}{c}P^{-1}(z)A(z)P(z)-P^{-1}(z)\dot{P}(z)\right],$$

where the diagonal matrix is

$$(4.11a) \qquad D(z) \equiv \left(\left[i\,\frac{\omega}{c}\,\lambda_j+r_{jj}\right]\delta_{jk}\right)$$

and the zero-diagonal matrix is

$$(4.11b) \qquad N(z) \equiv \left(r_{jk}(z)\left[1-\delta_{jk}\right]\right).$$

With the above definitions the solution (4.6) becomes

- 11 -

$$U(z) = \Omega \left\{ D+N \right\} U_0$$

$$(4.12) \qquad = \exp\left[\int_{z_0}^{z} D(x)dx\right] \Omega \left\{ \exp\left[-\int_{z_0}^{x} D(\xi)d\xi\right] N(x) \exp\left[\int_{z_0}^{x} D(\xi)d\xi\right] \right\} U_0$$

(see Appendix I for the identities used). To simplify further, we introduce the matrix $M(x)$ with elements

$$(4.13) \quad m_{ij}(x) = [1-\delta_{ij}]\left\{ r_{ij}(x)\exp\left[\int_{z_0}^{x}[r_{ii}(\xi)-r_{jj}(\xi)]d\xi\right]\right\} \exp\left[i\,\frac{\omega}{c}\int_{z_0}^{x}[\lambda_i(\xi)-\lambda_j(\xi)]d\xi\right].$$

This matrix is the argument of the matrizant of the final equation (4.12) which has been written explicitly by means of equations (4.11) and (I.2) and (I.4). Letting the elements of this matrizant be $\Omega_{ij}(z)$ we have, from equations (4.12), (4.13) and (I.1),

$$(4.14) \quad \Omega_{ij}(z) = \delta_{ij} + \int_{z_0}^{z}dx_1 m_{ij}(x_1) + \sum_{k=1}^{4}\int_{z_0}^{z}dx_2\int_{z_0}^{x_2}dx_1 m_{ik}(x_2)m_{kj}(x_1) + \cdots.$$

Finally we introduce the column matrix $C(z_0,z)$ with the four elements $c_i(z_0,z)$ defined by

$$(4.15) \qquad c_i(z_0,z) = \sum_{j=1}^{4}\Omega_{ij}(z)u_j(z_0);\; i = 1,2,3,4.$$

From equations (4.12) to (4.15) we obtain for the individual characteristic waves

$$(4.16) \qquad u_j(z) = \exp\left(\int_{z_0}^{z}r_{jj}(x)dx\right)\cdot \exp\left(i\,\frac{\omega}{c}\int_{z_0}^{z}\lambda_j(x)dx\right)\cdot c_j(z_0,z);$$

$$j = 1,2,3,4.$$

4a. <u>Interpretation of Characteristic Wave Solution.</u> Each characteristic wave (4.16) consists of three factors. The second factors in those four waves are

$$\exp\left[i\,\frac{\omega}{c}\int_{z_0}^{z}\lambda_j(x)dx\right]: \qquad j = 1,2,3,4;$$

these reveal the 'wavelike' behavior of the characteristic waves and thus are
called the "wave factors". They are all distinct since the eigenvalues $\lambda_j(x)$
have been assumed unequal. Let two of these factors, say those containing
$\lambda_1(x)$ and $\lambda_3(x)$ represent rising waves and the remaining two downcoming waves.
The $\lambda_1(x)$ and $\lambda_2(x)$ wave factors shall be called "ordinary wave factors"
and the remaining two "extraordinary wave factors". Thus $u_1(z)$ and $u_2(z)$
are the rising and the downcoming ordinary characteristic waves respectively,
while $u_3(z)$ and $u_4(z)$ are the rising the downcoming extraordinary characteristic waves respectively. This is the usual ionospheric terminology which
is justified in Sections 9 and 10, where specific cases are treated.

The first factor of the solution (4.16),

$$\exp\left[\int_{z_0}^{z} r_{jj}(x)dx\right], \quad j = 1,2,3,4,$$

yields a W.K.B. behavior of the characteristic waves. This is shown explicitly for the troposphere in [2] and for the two specific ionospheric cases in
Sections 9 and 10. In all three cases it is seen that $r_{jj}(x)$ contains the
negative logarithmic derivative of $\lambda_j^{1/2}(x)$. In the more general case it has
been shown (see [2], Appendix III) that some such logarithmic derivative is
always present and thus represents a generalized W.K.B. behavior.

The factors $c_i(z_0,z)$ in the solution are called "continuous scattering
factors". They describe the continuous multiple reflection which is expected
in an inhomogeneous medium. Besides this expected phenomenon, the anisotropy
causes a change of type (i.e., ordinary into extraordinary and vice versa)
upon reflection as well as during continuous transmission. This change of
type which occurs in the direction of propagation shall be called a " transi-

Equations (4.13) and (4.14) indicate that $\Omega_{ij}(z)$ represents the
total contribution to a λ_i-wave factor, by a λ_j-wave factor, by all possible

multiple continuous reflections and transitions and combinations of the two.
More explicitly in equation (4.13) we may introduce

$$(4.17) \qquad R_{ij}(x) = r_{ij}(x) \exp\left[\int_{z_o}^{x} (r_{ij}(\xi) - r_{jj}(\xi))d\xi\right], \quad i \neq j,$$

which are interpreted as continuous reflection and transition coefficients
for λ_j-waves changing into λ_i-waves. From the previous description of the
characteristic wave factors, the above coefficients may be classified as
follows:

		Reflection Coefficients	Transition Coefficients
(4.18)	No Type Change:	R_{12}, R_{21}; R_{34}, R_{43}	—
	Change of Type:	R_{14}, R_{41}; R_{23}, R_{32}	R_{13}, R_{31}; R_{24}, R_{42}

This table together with Equation (4.17) constitutes an extension to anisotropic media of the usual Fresnel coefficients for isotropic media. Such
an extension has been mentioned by Bremmer [8], but who does not, however,
give explicit expressions; this is done here in Sections 9 and 10 for two
specific ionospheric cases.

As an example of the above description consider, say, $\Omega_{41}(z)$, the
contributions to the downcoming extraordinary wave, (λ_4-wave) originating
from the rising ordinary wave (λ_1-wave). From Equation (4.14) one of the
fourth-order terms in this sum is

$$\Omega_{41}(z) = \cdots + \int_{z_o}^{z} dx_4 \int_{z_o}^{x_4} dx_3 \int_{z_o}^{x_3} dx_2 \int_{z_o}^{x_2} dx_1 m_{43}(x_4)m_{31}(x_3)m_{12}(x_2)m_{21}(x_1) + \cdots$$

("Fourth-order" means that the number of continuous reflection and transitions
totals four.) From Equations (4.13) and (4.17) this term is observed to contain the reflection and transition coefficients R_{43}, R_{31}, R_{12} and R_{21} in that
order. This accounts for the following phenomena (see Figure 1): the rising
ordinary wave feeds by reflection the downgoing ordinary wave; this in turn

'eeds the rising ordinary waves; and by transition this feeds the rising extra-

rdinary wave, which finally feeds, by reflection, the downgoing extraordinary wave.

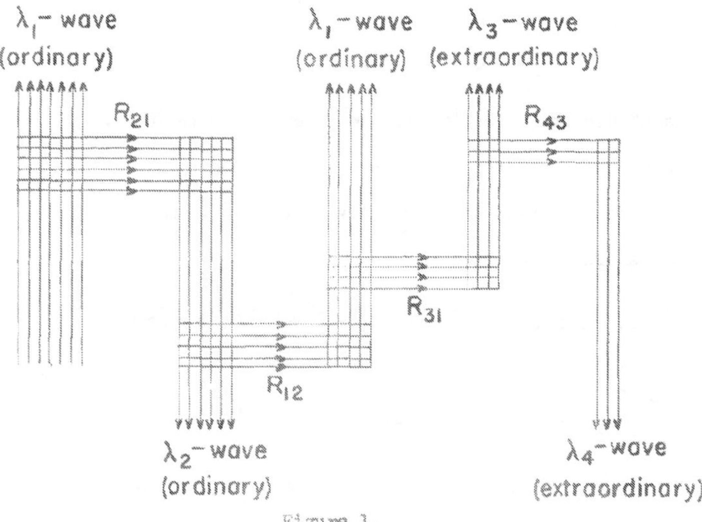

Figure 1.

The ordinary and extraordinary waves are said to be coupled if a wave

of one type feeds or produces a wave of the other type, that is, if an in-

dependently excited ordinary wave would give rise to an extraordinary wave

and vice versa. In general, this is the case for the ionosphere. However,

if those continuous reflection and transition coefficients which refer to

$$(4.20) \qquad (\tfrac{i\omega}{c} P^{-1}AP - P^{-1}\dot{P}) = \begin{pmatrix} - & - & 0 & 0 \\ - & - & 0 & 0 \\ 0 & 0 & - & - \\ 0 & 0 & - & - \end{pmatrix} \;,$$

where the dashes represent arbitrary functions, then there is uncoupling. In this case the fourth-order system reduces to two-second-order systems. There are some known ionospheric cases in which this happens [9], the homogeneous ionosphere being a trivial example.

4b. Polarization in the Ionosphere. Performing the indicated matrix multiplication in Equation (4.4) gives

$$(4.21) \qquad w_i(z) = \sum_{j=1}^{4} P_{ij}(z)u_j(z), \quad i = 1,2,3,4.$$

From definition (4.1) the $w_i(z)$ are seen to be propertional to the electromagnetic field components, and hence these components are linear combinations, with variable coefficients, of the four characteristic waves. If each characteristic wave is considered to belong to a separate (i.e., independently propagating) electromagnetic field we may then determine the polarization of the characteristic fields. Since $w_1(z)$ and $w_4(z)$ are the x and y components respectively of the electric field vector, and $w_3(z)$ and $w_4(z)$ are the corresponding magnetic field components, the polarizations become:

	Ordinary Wave		Extraordinary Wave	
(4.22)	Rising	Downcoming	Rising	Downcoming
E-polarization	$P_{11}(z)/P_{41}(z)$	$P_{12}(z)/P_{42}(z)$	$P_{13}(z)/P_{43}(z)$	$P_{14}(z)/P_{44}(z)$
H-polarization	$P_{21}(z)/P_{31}(z)$	$P_{22}(z)/P_{32}(z)$	$P_{23}(z)P_{33}(z)$	$P_{24}(z)/P_{34}(z)$

However, these ratios give only the projections of the polarizations in the
transverse plane, since, in general, the longitudinal field components do
not vanish. Further, the assumption of independently propagating characteristic waves holds only for true characteristic waves and must thus be re-
garded as an approximation in general. These " polarizations" apply only
to fields within the ionosphere, and there is no justification, at present,
for assuming that a wave which has come from the ionosphere will have a
polarization which is the limit of one of the above expressions. This
question is discussed further in Section 6.

Although eight seemingly different polarizations have been defined,
it is expected that they should reduce to at most four, with two pairs
differing only in sign. This is found to be the case for the problems
considered in Sections 9 and 10, although it has not been proved in general.

5. Reflection Levels

The solution of Section 4 has been obtained under the assumption that
$A(z)$ could be diagonalized at all points in the interval $z_o \leq z \leq z_1$. We
call a point at which diagonalization is impossible a "reflection level"
and proceed to justify the terminology and examine the nature of the solution
at such a point.

If $A(z)$ cannot be diagonalized then $\lambda I - A(z)$ must have non-simple elementary
divisors, and hence the characteristic equation (4.8) must have repeated roots.
Specifically, let us assume that $\lambda_1(z) = \lambda_2(z)$, and that the other pair
is distinct in some small interval, say $z' \leq z \leq ''$. It is then possible,
in general, to find a matrix $P(z)$ such that [7]

$$(5.1) \quad P^{-1}(z)A(z)P(z) = \begin{pmatrix} \lambda_1(z) & 1 & 0 & 0 \\ 0 & \lambda_1(z) & 0 & 0 \\ 0 & 0 & \lambda_3(z) & 0 \\ 0 & 0 & 0 & \lambda_4(z) \end{pmatrix} .$$

The procedure of Section 4, Equations (4.9) to (4.15), is now repeated with
the above choice for $P(z)$. The formalism is identical, and the main difference
occurs in equations (4.11) which now become

$$(5.2) \quad D(z) = \begin{pmatrix} \lambda_1(z) & 0 & 0 & 0 \\ 0 & \lambda_1(z) & 0 & 0 \\ 0 & 0 & \lambda_3(z) & 0 \\ 0 & 0 & 0 & \lambda_4(z) \end{pmatrix} ,$$

$$N(z) = \begin{pmatrix} 0 & \frac{i\omega}{c}+r_{12} & r_{13} & r_{14} \\ r_{21} & 0 & r_{23} & r_{24} \\ r_{31} & r_{32} & 0 & r_{34} \\ r_{41} & r_{42} & r_{43} & 0 \end{pmatrix}$$

where, as before, $(r_{ij}(z)) = -P^{-1}(z)\dot{P}(z)$. The $m_{ij}(x)$ defined by Equation
(4.13) differ explicitly only in $m_{12}(x)$ and $m_{21}(x)$, which become

$$m_{12}(x) = \left\{ \left[\frac{i\omega}{c} + r_{12}(x)\right]\exp\left(\int_{z'}^{x}[r_{11}(\xi)-r_{22}(\xi)]d\xi\right) \right\}$$

$$(5.3) \qquad m_{21}(x) = \left\{ r_{21}(x)\exp\left(\int_{z'}^{x}[r_{22}(\xi)-r_{11}(x)]d\xi\right) \right\} .$$

We obtain $\Lambda_{ij}(z)$ and $c_i(z_0,z)$ by using the new quantities in equations (4.14) and (4.15) and replacing z_0 by z' whenever it occurs. The ordinary characteristic wave solutions are obtained by using the matrizant identities and carrying out the matrix multiplication in equations (4.12) to (4.15) with the changes noted above and in equations (5.2) and (5.3). This yields

$$
u_1(z) = \exp\left[\int_{z'}^{z} r_{11}(x)dx\right] \cdot \exp\left[i\frac{\omega}{c}\int_{z'}^{z}\lambda_1(x)dx\right]\cdot c_1(z',z)
$$

(5.4)

$$
u_2(z) = \exp\left[\int_{z'}^{z} r_{22}(x)dx\right] \cdot \exp\left[i\frac{\omega}{c}\int_{z'}^{z}\lambda_1(x)dx\right]\cdot c_2(z',z).
$$

The expressions for $u_3(z)$ and $u_4(z)$ are similar but contain distinct characteristic wave factors.

Since the two ordinary wave factors of equations (5.4) are identical, no distinction can be made in this case as to the rising or downcoming character of the waves. It may be said that the two ordinary waves have become so strongly coupled as to be indistinguishable. Even if the medium were homogeneous (i.e., if $\hat{P}(z) = 0$ and hence $r_{ij}(z) = 0$) there would be coupling, as may be seen from the N matrix of equation (5.2). This coupling would not involve the extra-ordinary characteristic waves.

In inhomogeneous media, however, there is coupling of the extraordinary to the ordinary waves at a reflection level. This seems to contradict some of the literature (e.g., [10]) which states that extraordinary waves propagate unchanged in the neighborhood of an ordinary wave reflection level. Of course the coupling will be small for slowly varying media. Such coupling is also present in the neighborhood of an extraordinary wave reflection level.

The solutions indicated in the present section may possibly be used to onnect the solutions above and below the reflection region. An alternative conrection could be furnished by the solution expressed in equation (4.3) for the field components; we would then use the identity (I.5). A final possibility level and then to take the integrals along a path in the complex z-plane which avoids the reflection points. It should be remembered that the above connections refer to the exact wave solutions and not to their asymptotic forms. It is the latter problem which has received much attention in the literature [9].

6. Free Space Solution

Although the free-space plane wave solutions of Maxwell's equations are well known and easily obtained it is necessary for our purposes to find the form they take when the notation of the previous Sections is used; these solutions are then used in Section 7. Thus we consider Maxwell's equations (2.1) with $\overline{\overline{K(z)}}$ given by (2.3). Letting the field vectors have the form (3.3), we obtain by the analysis of Section 3

$$V_3(z) = -p\,I_2(z) + qI_1(z)$$

(6.1)

$$I_3(z) = pV_2(z) - qV_1(z),$$

and

(6.2)
$$\frac{dW(z)}{dz} = i\,\frac{\omega}{c}\,A\,W(z),$$

where $W(z)$ is defined in equations (4.1) and where

(6.3) $\quad A \equiv \begin{pmatrix} 0 & 1-p^2 & pq & 0 \\ 1-q^2 & 0 & 0 & pq \\ -pq & 0 & 0 & -1+p^2 \\ 0 & -pq & -1+q^2 & 0 \end{pmatrix}$

This matrix has the characteristic equation

(6.4) $\qquad |\lambda I - A| \equiv \left[\lambda^2 - (1-p^2-q^2)\right]^2 = 0.$

Thus the eigenvalues are

$$\lambda = \sqrt{1-p^2-q^2}$$

where the subscripts are chosen to conform with the descriptions given in previous Sections. There are two pairs of equal eigenvalues but it may be shown that the elementary divisors of $\lambda I - A$ are simple, provided that $p^2 + q^2 \neq 1$. We assume this to be the case. Then a diagonalizing matrix P and its inverse P^{-1} are

$$
P \equiv \begin{pmatrix} \lambda & 1-p^2 & pq & 0 \\ 1-q^2 & -\lambda & 0 & pq \\ -pq & 0 & \lambda & -1+p^2 \\ 0 & -pq & -1+q^2 & -\lambda \end{pmatrix} \; ;
$$

$$
(6.6)
$$

$$
P^{-1} \equiv \frac{1}{2} \begin{pmatrix} \lambda^{-1} & (1-q^2)^{-1} & 0 & pq\lambda^{-1}(1-q^2)^{-1} \\ (1-p^2)^{-1} & -\lambda^{-1} & -pq\lambda^{-1}(1-p^2)^{-1} & 0 \\ 0 & pq\lambda^{-1}(1-q^2)^{-1} & \lambda^{-1} & -(1-q^2)^{-1} \\ -pq\lambda^{-1}(1-p^2)^{-1} & 0 & -(1-p^2)^{-1} & -\lambda^{-1} \end{pmatrix} \; .
$$

The solution of the system (6.2) is now easily obtained by the extended Peano-Baker method of Section 4.

We introduce the new variables, $u_i(z)$, by the column matrix

$$
(6.7) \qquad U(z) = P^{-1}W(z).
$$

Since $\dot{P} = 0$, this matrix satisfies the equation

$$
(6.8) \qquad \frac{dU(z)}{dz} = i \frac{\omega}{c} \Lambda U(z),
$$

where by equations (6.3) and (6.6) $P^{-1}AP = \Lambda \equiv (\lambda_i \delta_{ij})$. The solution of the system (6.8) is

$$U(z) = \mathop{\Lambda}_{z_*}^{z} \left\{ i \frac{\omega}{c} \right\} U(z_*)$$

$$(6.9) \qquad = \begin{pmatrix} e^{i\frac{\omega}{c}\lambda(z-z_*)} u_1(z_*) \\[2ex] e^{-i\frac{\omega}{c}\lambda(z-z_*)} u_2(z_*) \\[2ex] e^{i\frac{\omega}{c}\lambda(z-z_*)} u_3(z_*) \\[2ex] e^{-i\frac{\omega}{c}\lambda(z-z_*)} u_4(z_*) \end{pmatrix},$$

where we have used the definitions (6.5), and $U(z_*) = P^{-1}W(z_*)$; z_* is an arbitrary point at which the field is assumed to be known. The field quantities $W(z)$ are, from equations (6.7) and (6.9),

$$(6.10) \qquad \begin{aligned} W(z) &= PU(z) \\ &= P \mathop{\Lambda}_{z_*}^{z} \left\{ i \frac{\omega}{c} \lambda \right\} U(z_*). \end{aligned}$$

This is the usual plane wave solution for free space.

The coefficient matrix (6.3), indicates that if $p = 0$ or $q = 0$ (i.e. if the wave is normal in the xy- or the xz- plane), then $V_1(z)$ and $I_2(z)$ are independent of $V_2(z)$ and $I_1(z)$. These two pairs of uncoupled field quantities are the familiar E-waves and H-waves, which can be excited independently. From the discussion of coupling in Section 4, it is seen that the ordinary and extraordinary waves are the analogues, in the ionosphere, of the usual E and H waves in isotropic media.

7. Ionospheric Reflection Coefficients

In order to find the ionospheric reflection coefficients we must solve the problem formulated after equations (2.4). To summarize briefly, equations (2.1) and (2.3) are to be satisfied for $z \geq z_1$ and $z \leq z_0 > 0$ and equations (2.1) and (2.2) are to be satisfied in the range $z_0 \leq z \leq z_1$. By separation of variables and the reductions indicated in equations (3.1) to (3.5) and (6.1) to (6.3) this problem is reduced to the systems (4.2) in the ionosphere, $z_0 \leq z \leq z_1$, and (6.2) for $z = z_0$ and $z = z_1$, and the radiation and incident plane wave conditions (3.7) and (3.8) respectively must hold in the free space regions indicated. With the above formulation we seek the electromagnetic field below the ionosphere, $z < z_0$, and in particular the amplitudes of the downcoming waves at $z = 0$.

By the analysis of Sections 4 and 6 the column matrices $W(z)$ which are proportional to the transverse electromagnetic field quantities, are found to be

$$(7.1) \qquad \begin{aligned} W_-(z) &= P_- U_-(z), & z &\leq z_0 \\ W(z) &= P(z)U(z), & z_0 &\leq z \leq z_1 \\ W_+(z) &= P_+ U_+(z), & z &\geq z_1 \end{aligned}$$

where

$$(7.2) \qquad \begin{aligned} U_-(z) &= \underset{o}{\overset{z}{\Omega}} \left\{ i\,\frac{\omega}{c}\,\Lambda_- \right\} U_-(0) \\[2ex] U(z) &= \underset{z_0}{\overset{z}{\Omega}} \left\{ i\,\frac{\omega}{c}\,\Lambda(z) - P^{-1}(z)\dot{P}(z) \right\} U(z_0) \\[2ex] U_+(z) &= \underset{z_1}{\overset{z}{\Omega}} \left\{ i\,\frac{\omega}{c}\,\Lambda_+ \right\} U_+(z_1). \end{aligned}$$

Here the $-$ and $+$ subscripts refer to quantities below and above the ionosphere respectively, and the matrices $P(z)$, $\Lambda(z)$, P_+, and Λ_+ are defined in Sections 4 and 6. Since both regions exterior to the ionosphere are free space we have $P_+ = P_-$ and $\Lambda_+ = \Lambda_-$.

Now we apply the first of the conditions (3.8) to $W_-(z)$ and use equations (6.6) and (6.9) (for $z_* = 0$), and the first of (7.2) to obtain

$$(7.3) \qquad \left\{ \begin{aligned} \lambda_- u_1(0) + pq u_3(0) &= A_1 \\ - pq u_3(0) &= A_2 \ . \end{aligned} \right.$$

Thus we have

$$(7.4) \qquad U_-(0) = \begin{pmatrix} A_1 + A_2/\lambda_- \\ u_2(0) \\ -A_2/pq \\ u_4(0) \end{pmatrix} ,$$

and the quantities $u_2(0)$ and $u_4(0)$ remain to be determined. The radiation condition (3.7) applied to $W_+(z)$ yields, in similar fashion

$$(7.5) \qquad U_+(z_1) = \begin{pmatrix} u_1(z_1) \\ 0 \\ u_3(z_1) \\ 0 \end{pmatrix},$$

where $u_1(z_1)$ and $u_3(z_1)$ are to be determined.

To obtain these four unknown constants we apply the continuity conditions (3.6) at $z = z_0$ and $z = z_1$:

$$W_-(z_0) = W(z_0)$$
$$(7.6)$$
$$W(z_1) = W_+(z_1).$$

Using (7.1) and (7.2) we obtain from the above equations:

$$\begin{aligned}
P_+ U_+(z_1) = W_+(z_1) &= P(z_0)U(z_1) = W(z_1) \\
&= P(z_1) \; \underset{z_0}{\overset{z_1}{\Omega}} \left\{ i \frac{\omega}{c} \Lambda(x) - P^{-1}(x)\overset{\bullet}{P}(x) \right\} P^{-1}(z_0)W(z_0) \\
&= P(z_1) \; \underset{z_0}{\overset{z_1}{\Omega}} \left\{ i \frac{\omega}{c}\Lambda - P^{-1}\overset{\bullet}{P} \right\} P^{-1}(z_0)P_- \; \underset{o}{\overset{z_0}{\Omega}} \left\{ i \frac{\omega}{c}\Lambda \right\} U_-(0),
\end{aligned}$$

or finally

$$(7.7) \quad \begin{pmatrix} u_1(z_1) \\ 0 \\ u_3(z_1) \\ 0 \end{pmatrix} = \left(P_+^{-1}P(z_1) \; \underset{z_0}{\overset{z}{\Omega}} \left\{ i \frac{\omega}{c} \Lambda(x) - P^{-1}(x)\overset{\bullet}{P}(x) \right\} P^{-1}(z_0)P_- \right)$$
$$\exp\!\left(i \frac{\omega}{c} \Lambda_-(z_0)\right) \begin{pmatrix} A_1 + A_2/\lambda_- \\ u_2(0) \\ -A_2/pq \\ u_4(0) \end{pmatrix} \quad .$$

This is a system of linear algebraic equations for the determination of the

$$u_2(0) = \frac{(b_{21}b_{44}-b_{24}b_{41})\,\dfrac{(A_1+A_2)}{\lambda_-} - (b_{23}b_{44}-b_{24}b_{43})\,\dfrac{A_2}{pq}}{(b_{22}b_{44} - b_{24}b_{42})}\,\exp\left[i2\,\frac{\omega}{c}\,\lambda_-(z_0)\right],$$

$$(7.8)$$

$$u_4(0) = \frac{(b_{41}b_{22}-b_{21}b_{42})\,\dfrac{(A_1+A_2)}{\lambda_-} - (b_{43}b_{33}-b_{23}b_{42})\,\dfrac{A_2}{pq}}{(b_{22}b_{44} - b_{24}b_{42})}\,\exp\left[i2\,\frac{\omega}{c}\,\lambda_-(z_0)\right].$$

Here the b_{ij} are elements of the coefficient matrix of equation (7.7). The transmission coefficients follow immediately if we substitute equations (7.8) in (7.7).

Part II. SPECIFIC CASES

8. Some Specific Formulations

Electromagnetic plane waves in the ionosphere have been shown, in Sections 2 to 4, to be of the form

(8.1)
$$\vec{\mathcal{E}}(x,y,z,t) = \vec{V}(z)\,\exp\!\left[-i\,\frac{\omega}{c}(ct-px-qy)\right]$$
$$\vec{\mathcal{H}}(x,y,z,t) = \vec{I}(z)\,\exp\!\left[-i\,\frac{\omega}{c}(ct-px-qy)\right] \ .$$

The six quantities $\vec{V}(z)$ and $\vec{I}(z)$ are determined by

(8.2)
$$V_3(z) = \frac{-1}{k_{33}(z)}\left[pI_2(z)-qI_1(z)+k_{31}(z)V_1(z)+k_{32}(z)V_2(z)\right]$$

$$I_3(z) = \left[p\,V_2(z) - q\,V_1(z)\right]$$

and

(8.3)
$$\frac{dW(z)}{dz} = i\,\frac{\omega}{c}\,A(z)W(z).$$

The matrices $W(z)$, $A(z)$ and the elements $k_{ij}(z)$ are defined in equations (4.1) and (2.2) (with (2.4)) respectively. A general form of the solution of the system (8.3) has been obtained in Section 4. In the present Section we consider "explicit formulations" of the problem of obtaining such plane wave solutions. We consider two directions of incidence of the plane wave, and with each of these, several orientations of the earth's magnetic field. For each case, we determine $A(z)$ as well as its characteristic equation and eigenvalues. The method of Section 4 could then be applied.

It should be noted that the characteristic equation in each of the following cases is just the usual fourth-degree equation of magneto-ionic theory for that case. The squares of the eigenvalues are the so-called ordinary and extraordinary dielectric constants. The elements $k_{31}(z)$, $k_{32}(z)$ and $k_{33}(z)$, which are required for a complete determination of the field, are not given here but may be obtained from equations (2.2) and (2.4).

In brackets, after the name of each case, are references to some papers in which this particular case has been considered.

A. Plane Waves Parallel to the y-axis: q = 0

In all such cases $A(z)$ has the general form

$$(8.4) \quad A(z) \equiv \begin{pmatrix} -a & \mu' & 0 & -c* \\ a & -a* & 0 & -\gamma* \\ \gamma & c & 0 & \beta' \\ 0 & 0 & -1 & 0 \end{pmatrix} ,$$

with the characteristic equation

$$|\lambda I - A| \equiv \lambda^4 + [a+a*]\lambda^3 + [aa*-a\mu'+\beta']\lambda^2 + [\beta'(a+a*)-(\gamma c*+\gamma*c)]\lambda$$

$$(8.5) \qquad\qquad + [(\beta'aa*-acc*)-(\gamma c*a*+\gamma*ca)-\mu')a\beta'+\gamma\gamma*)] = 0.$$

This equation becomes biquadratic, and may be easily solved, if

$$(8.6) \qquad \begin{aligned} a + a* &= 0 \\ \gamma c* + \gamma*c &= 0. \end{aligned}$$

The eigenvalues in this case are given by

$$\lambda^2 = \tfrac{1}{2}(a^2+a\mu'-\beta') \pm \tfrac{1}{2}\left\{(a^2+a\mu'-\beta')^2-4[2a\gamma c*-\beta'(a^2+a\mu')-(acc*+\mu'\gamma\gamma*)]\right\}^{1/2}.$$

(8.7)

The elements and the eigenvalues of tne matrix (8.4) are given below for
the indicated magnetic field directions.

1) Vertical Magnetic Field: $y_1 = y_2 = 0$ [11]

$$(8.8) \quad \begin{cases} a = a* = c = c* = 0 \\[4pt] a = \beta = 1 - \dfrac{X\delta}{\delta^2-y_3^2} \quad ; \quad \beta' = -\beta + p^2 \\[10pt] \gamma = -\gamma* = 1\,\dfrac{Xy_3}{\delta^2-y_3^2} \quad ; \quad \mu' = 1 - p^2\,\dfrac{\delta}{\delta-X} \end{cases} ,$$

$$\lambda^2 = \tfrac{1}{2}(a\mu'-\beta') \pm \tfrac{1}{2}\left\{(a\mu'+\beta')^2 - 4\mu'\gamma^2\right\}^{1/2}$$

11) Horizontal Magnetic Field: $y_3 = 0$ [5,8]

(a) Field along x-axis: $y_2 = y_3 = 0$ ("north-south' transmission
in magnetic equatorial regions):

$$.9) \quad \begin{cases} a = a* = \gamma = \gamma* = 0 \\[4pt] \alpha = 1 - \dfrac{X}{\delta} \\[10pt] \beta = 1 - \dfrac{X(\delta-X)}{(\delta^2-y_1^2-X\delta)} \quad ; \quad \beta' = -\beta + p^2 \\[14pt] c = -c* = i\,\dfrac{pXy_1}{(\delta^2-y_1^2-X\delta)} \;;\; \mu' = 1 - \dfrac{p^2(\delta^2-y_1^2)}{(\delta^2-y_1^2-X\delta)} \end{cases} ,$$

$$\lambda^2 = \frac{1}{2}(c\mu'-\beta') \pm \frac{1}{2}\left\{(c\mu'+\beta')^2 - 4ac^2\right\}^{1/2} .$$

(b) Field along y-axis $= y_1 = y_3 = 0$ ("east-west" transmission in gnetic equatorial regions):

$$.10) \quad \begin{cases} c = c* = \gamma = \gamma* = 0 \\[4pt] \alpha = 1 - \dfrac{X(\delta-X)}{(\delta^2-y_2^2-X\delta)} \\[10pt] \beta = 1 - \dfrac{X}{\delta} \quad ; \quad \beta' = -\beta + p^2 \\[14pt] a = -a* = i\,\dfrac{pXy_2}{(\delta^2-y_2^2-X\delta)} \;;\; \mu' = 1 - \dfrac{p^2(\delta^2-y_2^2)}{(\delta^2-y_2^2-X\delta)} \end{cases} ,$$

$$\lambda^2 = a^2 + \alpha\mu', \text{ and}$$
$$\lambda^2 = -\beta' .$$

<u>Normally Incident Plane Waves: $p = q = 0$</u>

In these cases $A(z)$ has the general form

$$.11) \quad A(z) = \begin{pmatrix} 0 & 1 & 0 & 0 \\ \alpha & 0 & 0 & -\gamma* \\ \gamma & 0 & 0 & -\beta \\ 0 & 0 & -1 & 0 \end{pmatrix} ,$$

th the characteristic equation

$$.12) \qquad (\lambda^2 - c)(\lambda^2 - \beta) - \gamma\gamma* = 0.$$

as for normal incidence the characteristic equation is always biquadratic,

For the indicated magnetic field directions we have:

   i) Vertical magnetic field $= y_1 = y_2 = 0$ [9], [5]:

$$(8.14) \quad \begin{cases} \alpha = \beta = 1 - \dfrac{X\delta}{\delta^2 - y_3^2} \\[4mm] \gamma = -\gamma^* = i\,\dfrac{Xy_3}{\delta^2 - y_3^2} \end{cases}$$

$$\lambda^2 = \alpha \pm i\gamma;$$

   ii) Horizontal magnetic field $= y_3 = 0$ [9], [5]:

     (a) Field along x-axis $= y_2 = y_3 = 0$:

$$(8.15) \quad \begin{cases} \gamma = \gamma^* = 0 \\ \alpha = 1 - X/\delta \\ \beta = 1 - \dfrac{X(\delta - X)}{(\delta^2 - y_1^2 - X\delta)} \\ \lambda^2 = \alpha \text{ and} \\ \lambda^2 = \beta; \end{cases}$$

     (b) Field along y-axis $= y_1 = y_3 = 0$:

$$\begin{cases} \text{same as equations (8.15) with } y_2 \text{ replaced by } y_1 \text{ and } \alpha \\ \text{and } \beta \text{ interchanged,} \end{cases}$$

   iii) Oblique magnetic field in yz-plane $= y_1 = 0$ [9], [10], [13]:

$$(8.16) \quad \begin{cases} \alpha = 1 - \dfrac{X\delta(\delta - X)}{\left[(\delta - X)(\delta^2 - y_3^2) - \delta y_2^2\right]} \\[4mm] \beta = \dfrac{\left[\delta^2 - y_3^2 - y_2^2 - X\delta\right](\delta - X)}{\left[(\delta - X)(\delta^2 - y_3^2) - \delta y_2^2\right]} \\[4mm] \gamma = -\gamma^* = i\,\dfrac{Xy_3(\delta - X)}{\left[(\delta - X)(\delta^2 - y_3^2) - \delta y_2^2\right]} \end{cases}$$

$$\lambda^2 = \tfrac{1}{2}(\alpha + \beta) \pm \tfrac{1}{2}\left\{(\alpha - \beta)^2 - 4\gamma^2\right\}^{1/2};$$

and

    iv) Oblique magnetic field in xz-plane: $y_2 = 0$:

same as equations (8.16) with y_2 replaced by y_1 and α and β interchanged.

9. Normal Incident Wave and Oblique Magnetic Field

The solution of the problem formulated as case B, iii) in the preceding Section shall be developed here. For this configuration we have $p = q = 0$ (i.e., normal incidence) and $y_1 = 0$ (oblique magnetic field in yz-plane). For the longitudinal field components we have, from equations (8.2), (2.2) and (2.4):

$$(9.1) \qquad \begin{aligned} I_3(z) &= 0 \\[2mm] V_3(z) &= \frac{-Xy_2}{\left[(\delta-X)(\delta^2-y_3^2)-\delta y_2^2\right]}\left[i\delta V_1(z)+y_3 V_2(z)\right]. \end{aligned}$$

The transverse components must satisfy

$$(9.2) \qquad \frac{d}{dz}\begin{pmatrix} V_1(z) \\ I_2(z) \\ I_1(z) \\ V_2(z) \end{pmatrix} = i\frac{\omega}{c}\begin{pmatrix} 0 & 1 & 0 & 0 \\ \alpha & 0 & 0 & \gamma \\ \gamma & 0 & 0 & -\beta \\ 0 & 0 & -1 & 0 \end{pmatrix}\begin{pmatrix} V_1(z) \\ I_2(z) \\ I_1(z) \\ V_2(z) \end{pmatrix} ,$$

where the elements $\alpha(z)$, $\beta(z)$ and $\gamma(z)$ are given explicitly in equations (8.16). This system can be reduced to two second-order coupled equations in a variety of ways and has been considered from that viewpoint by various authors [11, 13]. However, we use here the method of Section 4.

Thus we label the eigenvalues of the coefficient matrix, given by equations (8.16), as follows:

$$(9.3) \qquad \begin{aligned} \lambda_1 &= -\lambda_2 = \sqrt{\frac{\alpha+\beta}{2} + \sqrt{\left(\frac{\beta-\alpha}{2}\right)^2-\gamma^2}} \\[3mm] \lambda_3 &= -\lambda_4 = \sqrt{\frac{\alpha+\beta}{2} - \sqrt{\left(\frac{\beta-\alpha}{2}\right)^2-\gamma^2}} \end{aligned} \, .$$

Let us introduce the quantity $u(z)$ defined as

$$u(z) = -\left(\frac{\beta-\alpha}{2\gamma}\right) + \sqrt{\left(\frac{\beta-\alpha}{2\gamma}\right)^2 - 1}$$

(9.4)

$$= i\left\{\left[\frac{y_2^2}{2y_3(\delta-X)}\right] + \sqrt{\left[\frac{y_2^2}{2y_3(\delta-X)}\right]^2 + 1}\right\}.$$

Substituting (9.4) in (9.3) we obtain for the eigenvalues

$$\lambda_1^2 = 1 - \frac{X}{\delta+iy_3 u}$$

(9.5)

$$\lambda_3^2 = 1 - \frac{X}{\delta+iy_3/u}$$

Since, in general, $|u| \neq 1$, $\lambda_1 \neq 0$ and $\lambda_3 \neq 0$, the eigenvalues are distinct and the coefficient matrix may be diagonalized by a similarity transformation (i.e., equation (4.7)). Such a transformation is determined by

$$P(z) = \begin{pmatrix} u(z)\begin{pmatrix} 1 & -1 \\ \lambda_1 & \lambda_1 \end{pmatrix} & \begin{pmatrix} 1 & -1 \\ \lambda_3 & \lambda_3 \end{pmatrix} \\ \begin{pmatrix} \lambda_1 & \lambda_1 \\ -1 & 1 \end{pmatrix} & u(z)\begin{pmatrix} \lambda_3 & \lambda_3 \\ -1 & 1 \end{pmatrix} \end{pmatrix},$$

(9.6)

$$P^{-1}(z) = \frac{1}{2(1-u^2)}\begin{pmatrix} -u(z)\begin{pmatrix} 1 & \lambda_1^{-1} \\ -1 & \lambda_1^{-1} \end{pmatrix} & \begin{pmatrix} \lambda_1^{-1} & -1 \\ \lambda_1^{-1} & 1 \end{pmatrix} \\ \begin{pmatrix} 1 & \lambda_3^{-1} \\ -1 & \lambda_3^{-1} \end{pmatrix} & -u(z)\begin{pmatrix} \lambda_3^{-1} & -1 \\ \lambda_3^{-1} & 1 \end{pmatrix} \end{pmatrix}.$$

We now proceed as in equations (4.9) to (4.16) to find the solution. From the above matrices one obtains

$$- \left(r_{ij}(z) \right) \;=\; P^{-1}\,\frac{dP}{dz}$$

$$=
\begin{pmatrix}
\dfrac{d}{dz}\begin{pmatrix} \ell n\sqrt{\lambda_1(u^2-1)} & \ell n\sqrt{\lambda_1} \\[2ex] \ell n\sqrt{\lambda_1} & \ell n\sqrt{\lambda_1(u^2-1)} \end{pmatrix} & \dfrac{-\gamma}{\lambda_1}\left(\dfrac{d\,\ell n\sqrt{u}}{dz}\right)\begin{pmatrix} (\lambda_1-\lambda_3)^{-1} & -(\lambda_1+\lambda_3)^{-1} \\[2ex] -(\lambda_1+\lambda_3)^{-1} & (\lambda_1-\lambda_3)^{-1} \end{pmatrix} \\[6ex]
\dfrac{-\gamma}{\lambda_1}\left(\dfrac{d\,\ell n\sqrt{u}}{dz}\right)\begin{pmatrix} (\lambda_1-\lambda_3)^{-1} & (\lambda_1+\lambda_3)^{-1} \\[2ex] (\lambda_1+\lambda_3)^{-1} & (\lambda_1-\lambda_3)^{-1} \end{pmatrix} & \dfrac{d}{dz}\begin{pmatrix} \ell n\sqrt{\lambda_3(u^2-1)} & \ell n\sqrt{\lambda_3} \\[2ex] \ell n\sqrt{\lambda_3} & \ell n\sqrt{\lambda_3(u^2-1)} \end{pmatrix}
\end{pmatrix}.$$

The matrix $D(z)$ of equations (4.11a) has as diagonal elements the four quantities d_{ii}, where

$$\left.\begin{aligned} d_{11}(z) \\[2ex] d_{22}(z) \end{aligned}\right\} \;=\; \pm\,i\,\frac{\omega}{c}\,\lambda_1(z) - \frac{d}{dz}\,\ell n\sqrt{\lambda_1(u^2-1)}$$

(9.8)

$$\left.\begin{aligned} d_{33}(z) \\[2ex] d_{44}(z) \end{aligned}\right\} \;=\; \pm\,i\,\frac{\omega}{c}\,\lambda_3(z) - \frac{d}{dz}\,\ell n\sqrt{\lambda_3(u^2-1)}\,.$$

Thus $\displaystyle\bigcap_{z_0}^{z}\left\{D(x)\right\}$ has elements $\exp\left[\displaystyle\int_{z_0}^{z} d_{ii}(x)\,dx\right]$ given by

$$\sqrt{\frac{\lambda_1(z_0)(u^2(z_0)-1)}{\lambda_1(z)(u^2(z)-1)}} \quad \exp\left[\pm i\frac{\omega}{c}\int_{z_0}^{z}\lambda_1(x)\,dx\right]$$

(9.9)

$$\sqrt{\frac{\lambda_3(z_0)(u^2(z_0)-1)}{\lambda_3(z)(u^2(z)-1)}} \quad \exp\left[\pm i\frac{\omega}{c}\int_{z_0}^{z}\lambda_3(x)\,dx\right] \quad .$$

The elements of the matrix $M(z) = \left(m_{ij}(z)\right)$ become

$$-\frac{d\ln\sqrt{\lambda_1}}{dz}\begin{pmatrix}0 & e_{12}\\ e_{21} & 0\end{pmatrix} = \begin{pmatrix}m_{11} & m_{12}\\ m_{21} & m_{22}\end{pmatrix},$$

$$\sqrt{\frac{\lambda_3(z_0)}{\lambda_1(z_0)}}\left[\frac{\gamma(z)}{\sqrt{\lambda_1(z)\lambda_3(z)}}\frac{d\ln\sqrt{u}}{dz}\right]\begin{pmatrix}\dfrac{e_{13}}{\lambda_1-\lambda_3} & \dfrac{e_{14}}{\lambda_1+\lambda_4}\\[2ex] \dfrac{e_{23}}{\lambda_1+\lambda_3} & \dfrac{e_{24}}{\lambda_1-\lambda_3}\end{pmatrix} = \begin{pmatrix}m_{13} & m_{14}\\ m_{23} & m_{24}\end{pmatrix},$$

(9.10)

$$\sqrt{\frac{\lambda_1(z_0)}{\lambda_3(z_0)}}\left[\frac{\gamma(z)}{\sqrt{\lambda_1(z)\lambda_3(z)}}\frac{d\ln\sqrt{u}}{dz}\right]\begin{pmatrix}\dfrac{e_{31}}{\lambda_1-\lambda_3} & \dfrac{e_{32}}{\lambda_1+\lambda_3}\\[2ex] \dfrac{e_{41}}{\lambda_1+\lambda_3} & \dfrac{e_{42}}{\lambda_1-\lambda_3}\end{pmatrix} = \begin{pmatrix}m_{31} & m_{32}\\ m_{41} & m_{42}\end{pmatrix},$$

$$-\frac{d\ln\sqrt{\lambda_3}}{dz}\begin{pmatrix}0 & e_{34}\\ e_{43} & 0\end{pmatrix} = \begin{pmatrix}m_{33} & m_{34}\\ m_{43} & m_{44}\end{pmatrix},$$

where $e_{ij}(z) = \exp\left[i\frac{\omega}{c}\int_{z_0}^{z}\left[\lambda_1(x)-\lambda_j(x)\right]dx\right]$. Using the definitions (4.14)

and (4.15) we find that for the present case the solution, (4.16), takes the form

$$\mathop{u_1}_{2}(z) \;=\; \sqrt{\frac{\lambda_1(z_0)(u^2(z_0)-1}{\lambda_1(z)(u^2(z)-1}} \quad \exp\left[\pm\, i\, \frac{\omega}{c} \int_{z_0}^{z} \lambda_1(x)\, dx \right] \; \mathop{c_1}_{2}(z_0,z)$$

(9.11)

$$\mathop{u_3}_{4}(z) \;=\; \sqrt{\frac{\lambda_3(z_0)(u^2(z_0)-1}{\lambda_3(z)(u^2(z)-1}} \quad \exp\left[\pm\, i\, \frac{\omega}{c} \int_{z_0}^{z} \lambda_3(x)\, dx \right] \; \mathop{c_3}_{4}(z_0,z) \quad .$$

This solution has the interpretation given in Section 4a and 4b. The continuous reflection and transmission coefficients $R_{ij}(z)$, defined in (4.17) and (4.18), are here the coefficients of the e_{ij} in the matrix (9.10). There are essentially four of these, which we denote by

$$\rho_{oo}(z) \;=\; -\frac{d}{dz}\, \ell n \sqrt{\lambda_1(z)} \;,$$

$$\rho_{xx}(z) \;=\; -\frac{d}{dz}\, \ell n \sqrt{\lambda_3(z)} \;,$$

(9.12)

$$\rho_{ox} \;=\; \rho_{xo} \;=\; \left[\frac{\gamma(z)}{\sqrt{\lambda_1(z)\lambda_3(z)}} \; \frac{d}{dz}\, \ell n \sqrt{u(z)} \right] \frac{1}{\lambda_1(z)+\lambda_3(z)} \;,$$

$$\tau_{ox} \;=\; \tau_{xo} \;=\; \left[\frac{\gamma(z)}{\sqrt{\lambda_1(z)\lambda_3(z)}} \; \frac{d}{dz}\, \ell n \sqrt{u(z)} \right] \frac{1}{\lambda_1(z)-\lambda_3(z)} \quad .$$

Here $\rho_{oo}(z)$ and $\rho_{xx}(z)$ are the ordinary and extraordinary continuous reflection coefficients while $\rho_{ox}(z)$ and $\rho_{xo}(z)$ are the mixed reflection coefficients. The $\tau_{ox}(z)$ and $\tau_{xo}(z)$ are the continuous transition coefficients, which by definition are of mixed type. From equations (4.17), (9.10) and (9.12) we have

$$R_{12} = R_{21} = \rho_{oo}\,, \qquad\qquad R_{14} = R_{23} = \sqrt{\lambda_3(z_0)/\lambda_1(z_0)}\;\; \rho_{ox}\,,$$

(9.13)

$$R_{34} = R_{43} = \rho_{xx}\,, \qquad\qquad R_{41} = R_{32} = \sqrt{\lambda_1(z_0)/\lambda_3(z_0)}\;\; \rho_{ox}\,,$$

Thus the above classification is seen to check with the table (4.18). The quantities (9.12) aid in simplifying and interpreting the continuous reflection factors $c_i(z_o,z)$.

The solution (9.11) reduces to a slight modification of the usual magneto-ionic solutions when the coupling is small (or neglected). This result is obtained by assuming the $c_i(z_o,z)$ to be constants. The modification consists of the factor $(u^2(z)-1)^{-1/2}$, which in general varies to the same order as $\lambda^{-1/2}(z)$. In addition, this factor clearly shows that there is a turning point (or reflection level) wherever $u^2(z) = 1$.

Polarizations, defined in table (4.22) for the characteristic waves are evaluated from the $P(z)$ of equation (9.6): are

(9.14)

	ORDINARY WAVE		EXTRAORDINARY WAVE	
	Rising	Downcoming	Rising	Downcoming
E-POLARIZATION	$-u(z)$	$-u(z)$	$-1/u(z)$	$-1/u(z)$
H-POLARIZATION	$u(z)$	$u(z)$	$-1/u(z)$	$-1/u(z)$

There are essentially two kinds of polarization, the ordinary, $u(z)$ and the extraordinary, $1/u(z)$. These quantities were first derived in a more direct manner by Rydbeck [32]; (see his work for a more detailed discussion). The above table shows that the electric and magnetic polarizations are 180° out of phase. However, it should be recalled that these represent the polarizations of characteristic waves assumed to be independently propagating and that such waves are not necessarily excited by a source outside the ionosphere.

10. Oblique Incident Wave and Vertical Magnetic Field

In exact analogy with the previous section we shall obtain here the solution for the configuration of the case (A.i.) in section 8. Thus we now have $y_1 = y_2 = q = 0$, and equations (8.2) become

$$I_3(z) = p\, V_2(z)$$

(10.1)

$$V_3(z) = i\,\frac{c}{\omega}\,\frac{p\delta}{\left[(1-p^2)\delta - X\right]}\,\frac{dV_1(z)}{dz}\quad.$$

Here we have eliminated $I_2(z)$ by means of the first equation of the following system, which determines the remaining field components:

(10.2)
$$\frac{d}{dz}\begin{pmatrix} V_1(z) \\ I_2(z) \\ I_1(z) \\ V_2(z) \end{pmatrix} = \frac{i\omega}{c}\begin{pmatrix} 0 & \mu & 0 & 0 \\ \alpha & 0 & 0 & 0 \\ \gamma & 0 & 0 & \beta' \\ 0 & 0 & -1 & 0 \end{pmatrix}\begin{pmatrix} V_1(z) \\ I_2(z) \\ I_1(z) \\ V_2(z) \end{pmatrix}\quad.$$

Here we have discarded the prime on the μ for simplicity. Equations (8.8) give the elements of the coefficient matrix explicite. This system (10.2) is almost the same as (9.2); however, the slight difference will be seen to cause a much greater complexity in the present results.

The eigenvalues are

$$\lambda_1 = -\lambda_2 = \sqrt{\frac{\mu\alpha - \beta'}{2} + \sqrt{\left(\frac{\mu\alpha + \beta'}{2}\right)^2 - \mu\gamma^2}}\quad.$$

(10.3)

$$\lambda_3 = -\lambda_4 = \sqrt{\frac{\mu\alpha - \beta'}{2} + \sqrt{\left(\frac{\mu\alpha - \beta'}{2}\right)^2 - \mu\gamma^2}}\quad.$$

We introduce

$$u(z) \equiv \frac{\mu\alpha + \beta'}{2\gamma} + \sqrt{\left(\frac{\mu\alpha + \beta'}{2\gamma}\right)^2 - \mu}$$

(10.4)

$$= i\left\{-\left[\frac{p^2 y_3}{2(\delta - x)}\right] + \sqrt{\left[\frac{p^2 y_3}{2(\delta - x)}\right]^2 + \left[1 - \frac{p^2\delta}{(\delta - z)}\right]}\right\}\quad,$$

and then the eigenvalues become

-36-

The diagonalizing matrices

$$P(z) = \begin{pmatrix} u(z)\begin{pmatrix} 1 & -1 \\ \lambda_1/\mu & \lambda_1/\mu \end{pmatrix} & (\mu)\begin{pmatrix} 1 & -1 \\ \lambda_3/\mu & \lambda_3/\mu \end{pmatrix} \\[2em] \begin{pmatrix} \lambda_1 & \lambda_1 \\ -1 & 1 \end{pmatrix} & u(z)\begin{pmatrix} \lambda_3 & \lambda_3 \\ -1 & 1 \end{pmatrix} \end{pmatrix}$$

(10.6)   and

$$P^{-1}(z) = \frac{1}{2(\mu-u^2)}\begin{pmatrix} u(z)\begin{pmatrix} 1 & \mu/\lambda_1 \\ -1 & \mu/\lambda_1 \end{pmatrix} & (\mu)\begin{pmatrix} \lambda_1^{-1} & -1 \\ \lambda_1^{-1} & 1 \end{pmatrix} \\[2em] \begin{pmatrix} 1 & \mu/\lambda_3 \\ -1 & \mu/\lambda_3 \end{pmatrix} & u(z)\begin{pmatrix} \lambda_3^{-1} & -1 \\ \lambda_3^{-1} & 1 \end{pmatrix} \end{pmatrix}$$

From these matrices we compute

$$- r_{ij}(z) \equiv P^{-1}\dot{P}$$

$$= \begin{pmatrix} \frac{d}{dz}\begin{pmatrix} \ell n\sqrt{\frac{\lambda_1}{\mu}(u^2-\mu)} & \ell n\sqrt{\lambda_1} \\[1.5em] \ell n\sqrt{\lambda_1} & \ell n\sqrt{\frac{\lambda_1}{\mu}(u^2-\mu)} \end{pmatrix} & \frac{-\mu\gamma}{\lambda_1}\left(\frac{d\,\ell n\sqrt{u}}{dz}\right)\begin{pmatrix} (\lambda_1-\lambda_3)^{-1} & -(\lambda_1+\lambda_3)^{-1} \\[1.5em] -(\lambda_1+\lambda_3)^{-1} & (\lambda_1-\lambda_3)^{-1} \end{pmatrix} \\[3em] \frac{-\gamma}{\lambda_3}\frac{d\,\ell n\sqrt{u}}{dz}\begin{pmatrix} (\lambda_1-\lambda_3)^{-1} & (\lambda_1+\lambda_3)^{-1} \\[1.5em] (\lambda_1+\lambda_3)^{-1} & (\lambda_1-\lambda_3)^{-1} \end{pmatrix} & \frac{d}{dz}\begin{pmatrix} \ell n\sqrt{\lambda_3(u^2-\mu)} & \ell n\sqrt{\lambda_3} \\[1.5em] \ell n\sqrt{\lambda_3} & \ell n\sqrt{\lambda_3(u^2-\mu)} \end{pmatrix} \end{pmatrix}$$

(10.7)

$$+ \frac{1}{u^2-\mu}\frac{d\,\ell n\sqrt{u}}{dz}\begin{pmatrix} -u^2\begin{pmatrix} 0 & 1 \\ 1 & 0 \end{pmatrix} & \mu u\begin{pmatrix} 1 & -1 \\ -1 & 1 \end{pmatrix} \\[2em] u\frac{\lambda_1}{\lambda_3}\begin{pmatrix} 1 & 1 \\ 1 & 1 \end{pmatrix} & \mu\begin{pmatrix} 0 & 1 \\ 1 & 0 \end{pmatrix} \end{pmatrix} .$$

The diagonal elements of $i \frac{\omega}{c} \Lambda - P^{-1} \dot{P}$ become

$$\left.\begin{array}{c} d_{11} \\[2em] d_{22} \end{array}\right\} = \pm\, i\, \frac{\omega}{c}\, \lambda_1 - \frac{d}{dz}\, \ell n \sqrt{\frac{\lambda_1}{\mu}\,(u^2 - \mu)}$$

(10.8)

$$\left.\begin{array}{c} d_{33} \\[2em] d_{44} \end{array}\right\} = \pm\, i\, \frac{\omega}{c}\, \lambda_3 - \frac{d}{dz}\, \ell n \sqrt{\lambda_3 (u^2 - \mu)}$$

The matrizant $\overset{z}{\underset{z_o}{\Omega}} \left\{ D \right\}$ of this diagonal matrix has the elements

$$\sqrt{\frac{\mu(z)}{\mu(z_o)}}\ \sqrt{\frac{\lambda_1(z_o)\left[u^2(z_o) - \mu(z_o)\right]}{\lambda_1(z)\left[u^2(z) - \mu(z)\right]}}\ \exp\left[\pm\, i\, \frac{\omega}{c} \int_{z_o}^{z} \lambda_1(x)\,dx\right]$$

(10.9)

$$\sqrt{\frac{\lambda_3(z_o)\left[u^2(z_o) - \mu(z_o)\right]}{\lambda_3(z)\left[u^2(z) - \mu(z)\right]}}\ \exp\left[\pm\, i\, \frac{\omega}{c} \int_{z_o}^{z} \lambda_3(x)\,dx\right] \, .$$

From equations (10.7) and (10.9) the matrix $M(z)$ defined by (4.13) is obtained as

$$(10.10) \qquad M(z) = \left(m'_{ij}(z)\right) - \frac{1}{u^2 - \mu}\, \frac{d\,\ell n \sqrt{u}}{dz}\, \left(S_{ij}\right) ,$$

where

$$S_{11} = -\mu^2 \begin{pmatrix} 0 & e_{12} \\[1.5em] e_{21} & 0 \end{pmatrix}$$

$$S_{12} = \sqrt{u(z_o)}\ \sqrt{\frac{\lambda_3(z_o)}{\lambda_1(z_o)}}\ \sqrt{\mu}\,u\ \sqrt{\frac{\lambda_1(z)}{\lambda_3(z)}} \begin{pmatrix} e_{13} & -e_{14} \\[1.5em] -e_{23} & e_{24} \end{pmatrix} ,$$

$$s_{21} = \frac{1}{\sqrt{u(z_0)}} \sqrt{\frac{\lambda_1(z_0)}{\lambda_3(z_0)}} \left[\sqrt{\mu} - u \sqrt{\frac{\lambda_1(z)}{\lambda_3(z)}} \right] \begin{pmatrix} e_{31} & e_{32} \\ e_{41} & e_{42} \end{pmatrix},$$

$$s_{22} = \mu \begin{pmatrix} 0 & e_{34} \\ e_{43} & 0 \end{pmatrix} ;$$

$$m'_{11} = m_{11} , \quad m'_{22} = m_{22} ,$$

$$m'_{12} = \sqrt{\mu(z_0)} \, \sqrt{\mu(z)} \, m_{12} ,$$

$$m'_{21} = \frac{\sqrt{\mu(z)}}{\sqrt{\mu(z_0)}} \, m_{21} .$$

The m_{ij} are defined as in (9.10) and $e_{ij} = \exp\left[i \frac{\omega}{c} \int_{z_0}^{z} \left[\lambda_i(x) - \lambda_j(x) \right] dx \right].$

The solution and the continuous reflection and transition coefficients may now be easily obtained as in Section 9. It should first be noted that the expressions of the present Section reduce to those of the previous Section if we set $\mu(z) \equiv 1$. This was to be expected, since the systems (9.2) and (10.2) then become formally identical. The scattering coefficients are all sums of essentially the previous expressions plus terms due to the inhomogeneity of $\mu(z)$:

$$\rho_{oo}(z) = -\frac{d}{dz} \ln \sqrt{\lambda_1(z)} + \frac{u^2}{u^2 - \mu} \frac{d}{dz} \ln \sqrt{\mu(z)}$$

(10.11)

$$\rho_{ox}(z) = \rho_{xo}(z) = \sqrt{\frac{\mu(z)}{\lambda_1(z)\lambda_3(z)}} \left[\gamma(z) \frac{d}{dz} \ln \sqrt{u(z)} - \frac{\lambda_1 u}{u^2 - \mu} \frac{d}{dz} \ln \sqrt{\mu(z)} \right].$$

(10.12)

	ORDINARY WAVE		EXTRAORDINARY WAVE	
	Rising	Downcoming	Rising	Downcoming
E-POLARIZATION	$-u(z)$	$-u(z)$	$-\mu(z)/u(z)$	$-\mu(z)/u(z)$
H-POLARIZATION	$u(z)/\mu(z)$	$u(z)/\mu(z)$	$1/u(z)$	$1/u(z)$

Here there are four distinct polarizations, whose relationship to each other is somewhat surprising: the ordinary E-wave and extraordinary H-wave polarizations are the negative reciprocal of each other, and similarly for the other waves. The specific dependence of there polarizations on ionospheric properties may be obtained by using equations (10.4) for $u(z)$ and (8.8) for $\mu = \mu'$.

APPENDIX I

Definitions and Identities of the Modified Peano-Baker Method

For a square matrix $A(z)$ with bounded integrable elements $a_{ij}(z)$, the matrizant $\Omega_{z_0}^{z}\{A(x)\}$ is defined by

$$(I.1) \qquad \Omega_{z_0}^{z}\{A(x)\} \equiv I + \int_{z_0}^{z} A(x)\,dx + \int_{z_0}^{z} A(x_2) \int_{z_0}^{x_2} A(x_1)\,dx_1\,dx_2 + \ldots$$

Then the following identities can be proven:

$$(I.2) \qquad \Omega_{z_0}^{z}\{D(x)\} = \exp\left[\int_{z_0}^{z} D(x)\,dx\right] = \left(\delta_{ij} \exp\left[\int_{z_0}^{z} d_i(x)\,dx\right]\right),$$

where $D(x)$ is a diagonal matrix, and

$$(I.3) \qquad \Omega_{z_0}^{z}\{X+Y\} = \Omega_{z_0}^{z}\{X\}\, \Omega_{z_0}^{z}\left\{\Omega_{z_0}^{z-1}\{X\}\, Y\, \Omega_{z_0}^{z}\{X\}\right\},$$

where X and Y are square matrices of the same order. The inverse of any matrizant is

$$(I.4) \qquad \Omega_{z_0}^{z-1}\{A(x)\} = \Omega_{z}^{z_0}\{A(z)\}\,.$$

Another useful relationship is

$$(I.5) \qquad \Omega_{z_0}^{z}\{A(x)\} = \Omega_{\xi}^{z}\{A(x)\}\, \Omega_{z_0}^{\xi}\{A(x)\}\,.$$

BIBLIOGRAPHY

[1]   R.K. Luneberg: Propagation of Electromagnetic Waves, Notes;
      New York University, 1947.

[2]   H.B. Keller and J.B. Keller: On Systems of Linear Ordinary
      Differential Equations, Res. Rep number EM-33, Mathematics
      Research Group, New York University, Washington Square
      College of Arts and Science, 1951.

[3]   C.Th. F. Van Der Wyck: Uitbreiding Von Electromagnetischa Golven
      In Een Medium Met Veranderlijke Electrische Eigenschappen Bij
      Inachtneming van Een Magnetisch veld, Thesis, A.J. Mulder, 1946.

[4]   N. Marcuvitz: Waveguide Handbook; McGraw-Hill, New York, 1950.

[5]   H.G. Booker: Oblique Propagation of Electromagnetic Waves in a
      Slowly-Varying Non-Isotropic Medium; Proc. Roy. Soc.
      A, 155, 235-257, 1936.

[6]   C.C. Mac Duffee: The Theory of Matrices; Chelsea Pub. Co.
      N. Y. 1946. (p. 104).

[7]   J.H.M. Wedderburn: Lectures on Matrices; N.Y. Am. Math. Soc.,
      1934, Colloq. Publications, v. 17.

[8]   H. Bremmer: Terrestrial Radio Waves; Elsevier Pub. Co. Inc;
      1949 (Chap XI, Par. 6).

[9]   O.E.H. Rydbeck: On the Propagation of Waves in an Inhomogeneous
      Medium; Trans. of Chalmers Univ. of Tech., No. 74, 1948.

[10] V.L. Ginsburg: On the Influence of the Terrestrial Magnetic
      Field on the Reflection of Radio Waves From the Ionosphere;
      Journal of Physics (U.S.S.R.) Vol VII, No. 6, 1943.

[11] M.V. Wilkes: Oblique Reflection of Very Long Wireless Waves
      From the Ionosphere; Proc. Roy. Soc., 187, 130-147, 1947.

[12] K. Forsterling, Die Ausbreitung Electromagnetischer Wellen in
      einem geschichteten Medium unter der Mitwirkung eines
      Magnetfeldes bei schiefer Inzidenz, Arch. der elektro.
      Ubertr. 3, 115-120; 1949.

[13] J. Shmoys: Low-Frequency Propagation in an Exponential Ionospheric
      Layer; Res. Rep. number EM-51, Math. Res. Group, New York
      University, Washington Square College of Arts and Science, 1953.

www.ingramcontent.com/pod-product-compliance
Lightning Source LLC
Chambersburg PA
CBHW061102050726
47592CB00004B/1787